BOOKS BY
REYNOLDS PRICE

VITAL PROVISIONS   1982

THE SOURCE OF LIGHT   1981

A PALPABLE GOD   1978

EARLY DARK   1977

THE SURFACE OF EARTH   1975

THINGS THEMSELVES   1972

PERMANENT ERRORS   1970

LOVE AND WORK   1968

A GENEROUS MAN   1966

THE NAMES AND FACES OF HEROES   1963

A LONG AND HAPPY LIFE   1962

VITAL
PROVISIONS

REYNOLDS
PRICE

VITAL
PROVISIONS

NEW YORK

ATHENEUM

1982

Some of these poems appeared, in earlier forms, in the following places:

ALBONDOCANI PRESS *Angel, Anniversary, Archaic Torso of Apollo,
   Christ Child's Song at the End of the Night, Leaving the Island*
THE AMERICAN REVIEW *At the Gulf*
THE ARCHIVE *Black Water*
THE CAROLINA QUARTERLY *Man and Faun, Naked Boy*
ENCOUNTER *I Say of Any Man*
THE GEORGIA REVIEW *Divine Propositions*
THE MASSACHUSETTS REVIEW *The Dream of Lee*
THE ONTARIO REVIEW *Ascension, Reparation, Resurrection, Seafarer*
PALAEMON PRESS *The Dream of a House, Instruction, Pure Boys
   and Girls, Sleeping Wife*
PERMANENT ERRORS *The Alchemist*
POETRY *The Annual Heron, Pictures of the Dead, Rescue*
PRIVATE GREETINGS AND A BROADSIDE *Annunciation, Cumaean Song, For
   Leontyne Price after Ariadne*
QUESTION AND ANSWER *Dead Girl*
SOUTHERN REVIEW *Bethlehem—Cave of the Nativity, Jerusalem—Calvary,
   To My Niece*

Library of Congress Cataloging in Publication Data

Price, Reynolds, 1933–
     Vital provisions.

     I. Title.
PS3566.R54V5   1982   811'.54   82–71255
ISBN 0–689–11322–6
ISBN 0–689–11323–4 (pbk.)

Published simultaneously in Canada by McClelland and Stewart Ltd
Composed and printed by Heritage Printers, Inc.,
Charlotte, North Carolina
Bound by The Delmar Company, Charlotte, North Carolina
Designed by Harry Ford
First Edition

The earliest of these poems was completed in 1961, the latest in 1982. They are not, however, arranged in order of composition but in a sequence that means to clarify their relations with one another and with the lives from which they proceed. Nine of the fifty are results of my reading in languages that I know partially if at all. Thus they are free variations on originals whose concerns coincide so nearly with my own as to set them aptly in a personal sequence.   R. P.

CONTENTS

Contents

THREE

ANGEL

Every angel from its height
Sheds a pure though blinding light,
Intermittent noon and night.
Yet—or therefore—it deserves
Thanks, attentions, steady loves:
Every angel on its height
Burns itself, itself its light.
Burn, clear angel—I observe,
Thank, attend, attempt to serve.

ONE

THE DREAM OF A HOUSE

There seems no question the house is mine.
I'm told it first at the start of the tour—
"This is yours, understand. Meant for you.
Permanent." I nod gratitude,
Containing the flower of joy in my mouth—
I knew it would come if I waited, in time.
It's now all round me—and I catalog blessings
Tangible as babies: the floors wide teak
Boards perfectly joined, the walls dove plaster.
At either end a single picture,
Neither a copy—Piero's *Nativity*
With angel glee-club, Vermeer's pregnant girl
In blue with her letter. Ranks of books
On the sides—old Miltons, Tolstoys, *Wuthering*
Heights, Ackermann's *Oxford*. A holograph
Copy of Keats's "To Autumn." All roles
Of Flagstad, Leontyne Price in order
On tape, with photographs. Marian Anderson
At Lincoln Memorial, Easter 1939.
A sense of much more, patiently humming.
My guide gives me that long moment,
Then says "You've got your life to learn
This. I'll show you the rest."

I follow and the rest is normal house.
Necessary living quarters—clean,
With a ship's scraped-bone economy. Bedroom
Cool as a cave, green bath,
Steel kitchen. We end in a long
Bright hall, quarry-tiled—
Long window at the far end
On thick woods in sunlight.
The guide gives a wave of consignment—
"Yours"—though he still hasn't smiled.

I ask the only question I know—
"Alone?" He waits, puzzled maybe
(For the first time I study him—a lean man,
Ten years my junior, neat tan clothes:
A uniform?). So I say again
"Alone?—will I be here alone?"
Then he smiles with a breadth that justifies his wait.
"Not from here on," he says. "That's ended too."
But he doesn't move to guide me farther.
I stand, thinking someone will burst in on us
Like a blond from a cake; and I reel through
Twenty-six years of candidates,
Backsliders till now. Silence stretches
Till he points to a closed door three steps
Beyond us.

I cannot go. After so much time—
Begging and vigils. He takes my elbow
And pulls me with him to an ordinary door,
Black iron knob. I only stand.
He opens for me—an ordinary hall
Closet: shelf lined with new hats,
Coats racked in corners. In the midst
Of tweeds and seersuckers, a man is
Nailed to a T-shaped rig—
Full-grown, his face eyelevel with mine,
Eyes clamped. He has borne on a body
No stronger than mine every
Offense a sane man would dread—
Flailed, pierced, gouged, crushed—
But he has the still bearable sweet
Salt smell of blood from my own finger,
Not yet brown, though his long
Hair is stiff with clots, flesh blue.

The guide has never released my arm.
Now he takes it to the face. I don't resist.
The right eyelid is cool and moist.
I draw back slowly and turn to the guide.

*

Smile more dazzling than the day outside,
He says "Yours. Always."

I nod my thanks, accept the key.
From my lips, enormous, a blossom spreads
At last—white, smell strong as
New iron chain: gorgeous,
Lasting, fills the house.

THE DREAM OF LEE

I'm driving from Durham, North Carolina
To Lexington, Virginia to get General Lee.
He'll be spending two days at Duke University,
Meeting with students and giving one formal
Evening lecture. Time is the present—
Dull end of the seventies, unaccustomed
Relative peace in a world where
Danger is individual again:
Mad or malevolent single bodies
Of human beings no stronger than we,
Hurtling in dark (or broad daylight)
Through the final membrane that has kept us ourselves—
But nothing seems strange in the General's lasting
Well over a century past Appomattox.
The strangeness inheres in the land I speed through—
Hills hid in pines big as old redwoods,
No soul in sight for the whole four hours:
Vacuum containing just me and this quiet,
Though round every bend I expect some
Glittering messenger to hail me with urgent
News of grace, extinction or company.
None volunteers, today anyhow;
And at three o'clock I pull up behind
The President's House at Washington College,
And the General emerges from a stable to greet me.
Meet would describe the moment more nearly—
He is dressed in a deep-blue suit,
Wide lapels, gold chain cross the vest;
And he offers his hand and says "Mr. Price"
With a still grave beauty as rare as the land
I've approached him through and as fevered with promise
Or threat to help. But he says no more
Then. He motions toward the house
And I follow him there. He seats me

In a rocker on the wide porch, facing
The chapel where his white tomb will be.
He says a good deal in the next
Quarter-hour, inside in the hall
(I've angled to see through the open door)—
It takes him that long to extricate himself
From the famously hypochondriac Mrs. Lee,
Who seems in her wheelchair the statue
Of Obstinate Triumph I'd rather expected
Him to be. From her I can hear
Only "Robert, Robert." From him only "Mary,
I'm pledged to return." When he comes out finally
With his small black country-doctor's satchel,
He's shed one or two of the skins of calm
And shows round his eyes those crevices helplessly
Opened on *appall*, the toothless mouth
Of utter loss, abandonment
That make Michael Miley's last photographs
Of him such satisfactory likenesses of Lear.
But he smiles slightly and says "Lead on."

I lead him back down through the same
Dazed country—vacancy parting
Silent as water to accept our journey,
Shutting silent behind us. But he never mentions
The emptiness; and I only speak
When spoken to, which—after an hour
Of decorous grooming, more small
Talk than I'd guessed him good for—
Is a level question poured straight
At my profile in the tone of courteous command:
"We know my story. I would like to know yours."
I don't imagine he means a curriculum
Of places, dates; but no story
Comes—none that seems mine.
So I drive us, not speaking, to the Carolina
Line when he faces me again. I try
Not to look, pretend the wide
Vacant road requires my total

7

Attention (he knows it doesn't).
He says "I would be grateful to hear."
Still not facing him, I say "Tell
Me" and smile at the road. I mean
My story and I think he's
Answered when he gives a slow rub,
With his palm in the air, over half the visible
Arc of our view and says "Something
Very much like this here."
I know he means the view, the element
That's borne our journey till now—patient
Broadbacked unworked beast—
And dodging his eyes, I know he's right
Though I don't think "Why?" or ask
Him to paraphrase his gesture or the land.
I say "Yes sir" and the one
Other thing he asks awhile later is
The size of my family. I say "It's here
On the seat beside you. I bivouac light,
Vanish at will." I rub my chest
And smile again. He says "Mrs. Lee's
Life stopped years ago," but by then
We're there.
    The next two days
I stand as his aide through duties he's agreed to—
Several history classes with excellent
Questions on the details of campaigns,
Struggles with Jeff Davis, agonies
Of choice. He wears his perfect blue
Suit and answers perfectly, perfectly
Consistently—seamless as a river rock,
As shut to entrance; yet tall in impotence
As old Chief Joseph or a captive pope.
We fall back on pleasantry in what few minutes
He has between stints; he eats alone
In a hotel coffee-shop.
      He's ready
At the curb when I call to take him
To his formal lecture; and as I approach

Down the evening street, it seems the strangest
Thing of all that no single
Passer on a crowded pavement gives any
Sign of seeing, much less
Recognizing a face as beautiful
As any human feasible vision
Of any god in charge of Fate
And Mercy—serene now, omniscient,
The flare of wildness quenched or banked.

I introduce him to the crowded hall
And, reaching my conclusion, know I've forgot
To ask him his subject; so I end by telling
The audience I'm sure it awaits
The lecture as eagerly as I.
When oceanic welcome subsides,
The General rises, steps to the lectern,
Slowly unties a black leather case,
Then looks back to me and says "I regret
Not telling you. I hope my changed
Plan will cause you no pain." I smile.
He doesn't. He faces his crowd and says
"I shall read from my poems tonight."
Slightly chilled, I think "*The Poems of Lee*—
Is there any such book?" Before I decide,
The great voice starts—"First a poem I composed
Two days ago for my friend Mr. Price."
He waits, puts a fist to his lips and coughs,
Then reads a poem one line long—
"*A country emptied by the fear of war.*"
I turn translucent with discovery,
Story told; then transparent as a glass
Anatomical man, a lesson for children—
All organs (less genitals) blasted
By white magnesium glare as every
Eye in the hall scans me, smiles.

THE DREAM OF FOOD

The room is dark and is all your body.
In the single buttress of late light strained
Through the porous roof, I see you are all—
You constitute space, the walls of space,
Air (I breathe clean safety)—yet
You're plainly yourself, recumbent below me:
Irregular glory of bone and rind,
Bronze island of hair.
                              I wait in the door—
Not quite afraid, hoarding a dim
Astonishment, unsure of having
Or wanting permission.
                              You stir your left
Arm, the entrance wall; it oars me
In. Fluid, I lie on the floor—your
Breast (you're larger than I by maybe
Half and warmer by maybe a full
Degree, this side fever).
I pause incredulous, crouched on the tide
Of respiration; then accept your will
And stretch my legs down yours. My thighs
Discover a yielding terrain in your fork—
Mounds, channels. I calmly know you
Are utterly strange—not father, mother,
Girl or boy, though your skin is the standard
Pliant leather I recall as human.
I doubt my purpose but lighten my weight
For your next requirement. You cup the crown
Of my head and press. It descends in an arc,
Hours or days; is stopped on the field
Between your sternum and the dark past your
Belly. Total night.
                              My mouth
Rests precisely in a bowl of flesh off-center

In your side. My dry lips scout—perfect
Rim, scar-slick; scooped
Sides, in the pit a complicated
Knot. I test it with my teeth—apparently
Flesh, apparently plaited in three
Equal strands round a denser
Core.
      It silently feeds me.
My tongue is bathed in more than spit.
I draw back. Your hand presses
Firmly again. I submit and am given
A thread of what I decide is nourishment—
Thinner than milk and mildly bitter
With occasional grains I grind to paste.
In maybe a year I rise enough to thank you.
You press then with mammoth urgency, saying
"Never leave."
      I don't but endlessly
Consume your gift, growing at a glacial
Rate of my own and seeing each dawn
That the nearest wall is all your eyes,
All lashed like horsetails and flicking in random
Harmonies I scan for news
Of a world beyond us, if any
Survive.

SEAFARER

I can make one true song about myself—
Sing voyages, how I worked through Hell,
Tunneled my grief in bowels of ships
(Deep waves sucking) or above
When I drew dark watch at prow:
We sheering loud cliffs, feet locked in frost,
Heart scalded in grief, hunger ravening
Sea-wild soul.
   No man who draws land-luck can guess
How, crazed, I plowed desperate winter
Through rimey sea on exile road.
Stripped of kin, swathed in ice,
I'd strain to hear past crashing wave
And sometime catch swan call for solace,
Gannet, curlew for company,
Gull's caw for drink.
Storm pounded stone, cold tern answered,
Tattered horn-beaked eagle screamed,
But no kind kin warmed harassed heart.
So he who tastes in guarded towns
Glee of wine, homebound pride,
Who never treks bitter trails—
How can he guess how hard I rode
When forced to take sea's long path
Through night, north snow, all shore ice-barred
In stinging hail, coldest seed?
   Yet now my heart drums out thought
To taste again steep salt waves.
Famished heart yearns to fare
Forward toward homes of strangers,
Stranger lands—though can there be
Man so grand (free with gifts,
Flushed with youth, brave in deed,
Loved by his lord) that will not

Always dread his sail toward
What God dooms? For him can be
No thought of harp, winning of rings,
Joy in woman, joy in world—
Only waves. He who's sailed
Will long to sail.
   Trees burst with bloom, towns with beauty,
Fields freshen, life hastens—
All things drive eager soul
To wander, him who dreams of flood.
So cuckoo moans, summer's scout;
Sings harsh sorrow into hearts.
Men lapped in ease never know
What wretches know on exile road.
Still my mind roams past my heart.
My dreaming now on ocean flood
Roams wide—whale haunts,
Earth's skin—comes back
Unfed. Lone flier cries,
Whets heart for whale's way,
Ocean's breast, because God's joys
Weigh more with me than this dead loan
Of life on land.
   I here deny earth's riches last.
One thief of three will seize all men—
Plague, old age, hate—and only praise
From them who stay is fame past death,
Fame won in deeds from foes on earth,
Fiend in dark: fame among hosts of God,
Bright angels.
   Days are done now, all earth's glories.
Kings are gone now, Caesar's gone—
Great gold-givers cloaked in splendor,
Fallen, gone: old joys gone.
Weaklings last and swarm the world,
Win it with sweat. Pride is shamed.
Lords of life age and parch
Like other men in middle earth—
Ambush of age, face pales,

Hair grizzles, dim eyes watch
Sons of princes rendered to dark:
Flesh numb to sweets, hands still, mind still.
And though a brother long to sow
His brother's grave with gold—death-hoard
Guarded by him while he drew breath—
To go with him and his sinful soul
For help against God's awfulness,
He cannot now.
   Great is the Judge's awfulness—
World turns from it though he founded firm
Earth's skin and sky. Fool is he
Who does not dread his Lord.
Death will teach him.

after the Anglo-Saxon

QUESTIONS FOR A STUDENT

Nine months after I published a novel called
Love and Work, you woke me at 1 a.m. by phone
From Charlottesville; and we talked twenty minutes—
You talked; I held in groggy misery,
Unable to ask why, for this first favor,
You couldn't keep human time or what you wanted.
(I'd heard two years before when you were my student
That you'd been the youngest recipient
Of electroshock in Tarheel manic-depressive
Annals—a spunky file that holds its own—
But all I noticed as you talked a straight path
Through my thorny genre-course in the novel
Was the nails on your stub fingers,
Wolfed to the quick). And all I remember your saying
That night is "Do you really mean
What you say in the book?" I said I did—
True enough for the hour, I must have thought,
Though in my stupor I failed to ask
What you thought I said or why that mattered.

Three days later in afternoon light, you phoned
Your estranged wife; begged her to come back and—
When she refused for the umpteenth time—blew your brains out
With her on the line, a pause in your plea.

Even I don't assume the burden of that;
But ten years on, from a deep of my own
(Maybe no match for your Mindanao
But an honorable trench that sinks as I move),
May I ask these questions, awake at least?
Did I say Death and Silence?
If so was I wrong? If—as older books than mine
Predict—your agony lasts, can it help any way
If I offer here (late to be sure but in a safer genre)
This peace to your ruins, your bloody nails?

THE ALCHEMIST

Laughing, the chemist set the hot alembic
Where it could cool, fuming at his grin.
Now he knew what—simply—he would need
To force the thing he coveted to come:

Mind as girdling as the zodiac,
Free and sovereign but fiercely ruled,
Glomerate with power, a private sea;
Eons for seething down this crystal crib

—In which the monster of his yearning lay
(Got now, blind, by him on this blind night),
Prima Materia: rose past him to God

While babbling like a drunk he lay among
His magic-set, his priceless brittle gear,
And craved the crumb of gold he'd just now had.

after Rilke

AT THE GULF

The night I arrived you fed me grandly
At the new French restaurant—a hippie chef
Four thousand miles from Avignon (home),
The image of Courbet and as good at his work:
Champignons à la grecque, veal *cordon bleu*.
Then led me through alleys empty at ten—
Steaming palms, bananas, reek of shrimp—
To a pier from which you said we'd swim
Tomorrow (I'd flown since dawn to be here).
A strip of boardwalk ten yards long,
Not even a jetty, land itself roofed
In lazy confidence, well-placed apparently—
Six feet beneath us the hot brown Gulf
(The day had hit ninety, was only now dying)
Hunched impotent at pilings, force discharged
On reefs I'd seen from the plane, bone
Shield, gorget five miles out:
Making us the gorge.

Alone, grogged, we bulged round dinner
And—however dark and dead, too early to sleep—
Looked down dumb at the grateful sea,
Tamed shallow flank of the Mother, decrepit,
Whispering denials of her history.
Yet when I spoke first (to speak at all,
More than airport chatter, tabletalk),
I said "Not tomorrow. Forgot my armor."
You laughed—"It's safe, roped for swimmers"—
Then pointed outward. I strained to see,
Seine safety from night. None. Night.
The sounds—our breaths, water's helpless thanks
That we stood here for stroking. I said "Rope or nets?"
—"One rope."
                    I laughed. "And a sign saying

SHARKS KEEP OUT?"
                              You nodded.
"They can read. They know. Old enough to know."
—"Know what?"
                        "What's meat, what's bone." You faced me.
—"Which am I?"
                        Your turn to work; you smiled—
I was darker than you, you faced the light—
"Can't read," you said. "Not old enough."

—"You or I?" I thought but didn't ask.
We looked down again as though water were legible,
Engaged in clear signals, high-noon and help.
There was light—amber, the one you faced,
Bare bulb high on a shed behind me—
Invading the water till a thin layer phosphored,
Membrane the depth of muscles at work,
Achieving nothing, massage for plankton.

So you said "Ready?" to the water not me.
It had stroked me to a calm so anesthetic
That I never thought "For what?" but had stepped
To say "Yes"—to movement, reunion,
Repair, forgiveness, sleep—when you said
"No" and pointed with your turned face,
Dark, down. Below, a shape
Parallel to us in the burning water,
Slow and writhing without clear bounds,
Black, refusing light and name,
Condensation of crowded night.
Or—I knew at your left, one hand away—
A messenger sent with my answer to your "Ready?",
Coming since dawn (dawn of what?),
Arriving now. Five feet long, clearer
Since it rode higher toward us, undulant,
Still refusing, anonymous, black.
"What is it?" I said, also to the water,
And hoped "A saving dolphin in the wiggle-dance
Of bees" (saving who from what?).

*

When you knew, you turned again, bore the light,
Smiled—"One too young to read."
                                        "You're sure?"
I needed phylum, species, order.
—"A nurse shark prowling, a hungry baby."
It sounded—gone, message offloaded,
Return begun—and was instantly followed
By a second, leaner, priest to the oracle,
Interpreter, scourer.

He also writhed. Redundant—I'd learned,
Knew, looked up to ask "Do we swim?"
—"In the morning, after breakfast." You smiled.
—"Then there's time," I said to the water. "Grow."
You laughed. Our growing baby sank, offended.
You watched its mute plunge. Had you watched me,
Strained to see me (I was half to the light
For that one purpose, that you take the joke),
I was smiling in response, exhaustion, relief.

Idiot relief. For when we turned
(You took the first step, the lead toward home),
We turned again apart. Not at once—
One room, one struggle to join, stay joined,
But separate sleep where (drowned, in no light)
Smiles are less defense than a child's left hand,
Where we are no longer feeders but food
(Your cries woke me twice, your seizing hand),
Where meat and bone are nightly assaulted,
Rent past healing, abandoned diminished
In morning light.

LEAVING THE ISLAND

Even the coral reeks of us.
Alleys furred with rot burn our light.

We have done that kindness to several places—
Some of them common beds stripped quickly
Of visible spoor (invisibly salved, precious
With joy), actual cells cast off our juncture,
Fossil markers (to what? for whom?):
One block of a street, a shack on stilts,
An airport lobby where we passed like strangers,
A post-office table across which we spoke
(Spontaneous, hopeless) perfect words of total pardon—
Grand in memory as any in Genesis, *Cymbeline*.

The places are speechless with gratitude,
Heard by me.

ANNIVERSARY

Three years ago this week,
    You found an egg
Beside a hot crossroad,
    Pierced, drained but spared;
Intact—and no known hen
    For four, five miles.
How? Who? and Why? I took it
    As you gave it—
Silent gift—and propped it
    In a window.
Those years pass. Its eyeless
    Muddy gaze
Survives and says this much—
    "Function can change,
Form persevere,
    Fragile wholes
Be ruined yet outlast lives."

ATTIS

Borne over high seas in swift ship
To Phrygia, Attis urgent on hungry feet
Fled to black-shagged home of Goddess,
Rabid with need, mind choked on need.
There with flint unloaded his sex;
Then borne on lightness of her new freed body—
Fresh blood blotching earth, feet—
Seized light tambor (your tambor,
Cybele, Your mystery, Mother), struck it, rung it
In tense hand of snow, howled tight-throated
Song to sisters. "Up. Go. Scale
Crags of Cybele, clamber beside me—
Queen's prize herds hunting exile home,
Flock at my heels who've taken my lead
Through boiling surf on cruel sands,
Gouged Venus from thighs in excess loathing:
Feed Queen's heart with laughter of flight!
Now. To Cybele's piney home
Where cymbals crash, hard tambors answer,
Phrygian flutist blows curved calamus,
Maenads in ivy fling hot in ring,
Keen as they brandish sacred signs,
Where tramps of the Queen crowd to dance.
With me, beside me—run to join!"
When Attis—forged woman—summoned sisters,
Quivering tongues hissed Yes from dance,
Pocked cymbals crashed, tambors rang glad.
Ida's green sides bore clutching climb
After Attis—quickest, gasping, lost—
Still leader howling through thickening pines,
Unplowed heifer scared, lurching in harness.

*

There—spent—they dropped at Cybele's door,
Slept hungry blinding sleep that smoothed
Clenched minds, locked limbs.
But—dawn: gold Sun, His scalding eye
Struck air, packed ground, ferocious sea,
And Attis' sleep. Calmed, sealed eyes
Slit, Attis saw act and losses, saw
Puckering scars, raced in mind
To empty shores, wailed lost home.
"Home that made me, bore me, that I fled,
Hateful slave, to roam waste Ida—snow-choked,
Ice-ribbed caves of beasts, my own mind beast.
How?—where?—to reclaim you?
For this instant soul is sane, let eyes
See you once. Not again?—home,
Goods, parents, friends, market, ring,
Wrestling pit? Agony. Groan grinds groan.
What have I not been, what form not filled?—
I woman, cocked boy, boy-child, baby,
Crown of the track, oiled glory of the pit,
Warm doorsills ganged with friendly feet,
Garlands round me to deck my house
At dawn when I stood from my own wide bed:
Now priestess to gods, slavegirl to Cybele, maenad,
Scrap of myself, gored man, dry girl,
Chained—no hope—to green frigid Ida
With deer grove-haunting, rooting boar,
Each thin breath poisoned by memory."

Noise of her pink lips—news to gods.
Cybele, bending to lion at Her left, terror of herds,
Said "Now. Go. Hunt Attis
Toward Me. Drive him through woods till, mad, he heels;
Goes down appalled, lashed by your tail
To My ring where pines stagger at your voice."
Wild, She unharnessed yoke, lion crouched,
Roused rage, charged woods toward Attis, tender
By marble sea—slave, girlslave all his life.

*

Attis

Strong Goddess, Goddess Cybele, Goddess Lady of Dindymus—
Spare my house, Queen, from total fury.
Hunt others. Seize others. Others appall.

after Catullus

BETHLEHEM—CAVE OF THE NATIVITY

The air of this cave
Is actual substance,
Nearly transparent but grained
Like an oak wall or
Braided like water in a weir
Though still.

The blade of rust
That scores your tongue
Is atoms of iron—
Girl's blood on that rock
Where she spread,
Subliming at a constant rate
Two thousand years
Though tossed by flame
Of adoring lamps.

Taste slowly,
Drink.

Beyond this aromatic Greek monk
With the roll of toilet paper by his foot
(You must pay him to stand here)—
An altar on legs, beneath it a disc,
In the disc a hole.
                    If you've paid enough
(He names no sum), he'll say as you crouch
"Reach in. Golgotha.
Hole for cross."
                    Beware.
Eight empty inches, then live rock—
Cooling mouth, still raw
At the lip. One whole arm inserted
Would reach dead center.

PURE BOYS AND GIRLS

Pure boys and girls,
Diana's wards,
We praise her thus—
   Best seed of Jove,
Latona's child,
Cradled by her
Near Delian grove
(So You be Queen of Mountains,
Woods, Deep Glades,
Queen of Rivers crashing in their course),
Mothers in birth-groan
Call you Queen of Light,
Others Dark Lady,
Moon of Stolen Gleam.
Goddess, by months
You measure out our year,
Filling the honest farmer's house with store.
Holy—whatever name
You please to wear—
Save as you once saved
Romulus' big brood.

after **Catullus**

NIGHT SPEECH

In ten years of this
The most you've said
Is the odd "I'm glad"
To my declarations.
The rest is silence and
Its works—
Your silence, open as
Our window toward the sea
And above it your whole
Face charged
Again with my
Visitation: raft
Combusting in the night,
Moored to me.

TEN YEARS, FOUR DAYS

1. Petroleum dark.
   I pierce maybe you.
   Cries maybe your voice.

2. Greek cross—
   Equal arms, legs,
   Dense crown at the joint—
   Your thatch, my thorn.

3. You
   Through glaze
   Of maybe transport.
   Repeatable saint,
   Fugitive text.

4. Grinder.
   Who will eat this bread?

RESCUE

Something I never told you—I watched, hardly blinking,
Each moment of the morning you were nearly drowned
Or taken by moray, shark, barracuda
As you tested yourself in the half-mile channel
Between our room and Advent Island.

You know this much—that you walked down that morning
(A Monday in March) after breakfast on the beach,
Calm as a sleeper, to the hot smooth sea;
Fell forward on the water and dug your way
With no visible effort to a coral bone
Two hundred yards long: scene of nocturnal
Drinking parties and home to a huddle
Of scrub evergreens raided at Christmas
By natives of the larger bone, where we stayed.
You swam twenty minutes—past the odd flotilla
Of junk boats, sleek yachts—then walked up
Out of the sea as rested as a child at dawn,
Your back straight and steady, or like one of a number
Of maritime gods with grace to bestow
If they turn and look. You stood a few seconds,
Made two deep bows which were either obeisance
To what I could not see or simple stretches;
Then ran up the white beach, rounded the far end,
And vanished in cedars.
                                    I said to myself
Something very much like "The perfect soul"—
You, I meant, and *perfect* for me;
A statement untouched by the five years since—
Then turned to my reading, an hour of watching
Imagined souls secrete real lives
On my hands: peaceful joy.
                                              When I looked again
You were vanished still, no sight of you

On land or water. I think I felt
A quick chill in the morning,
Viscid bubble blown by a corpse.
I say *I think* when what I recall
Is I stood to watch and was clean again
Of the traces of you and well into dressing
When a workman knocked and entered to fix
The glass-door lock (we'd been open to passers).
I finished; he tinkered in admirable silence
Till he said—over some twenty feet between us—
"That child's a goner less he's stronger than he looks"
And aimed at the Gulf a finger cold
As the first hump of fear I'd ignored
Awhile back.
        I braced and came forward. You were midway
Between the island and me, stroking
Slowly. I could not see your face but you seemed
Safe enough. I asked the man "Why?"

He was back at his work and did not look again—
"Tide's turned against him and that's a shark channel."

In a minute's wait I confirmed the tide.
You were steadily draining-off to my left,
Nothing between you and Mexico but
Three hundred miles of thick green Gulf;
The sharks were a guess, though a native's guess
(Roughly half the American shark-attacks
Of the twentieth century occurred hereabouts).
I said "Who could help him?"
        He said "God Above
Or the U.S. Coast Guard if they're not at lunch"
And left, door fixed.
        The options were plain—
One, walk eight feet and phone the Coast Guard;
Ask them to rescue a single swimmer
In the tidal rush (it was sliding now
Toward some wide mouth in its hidden floor)
And risk your refusal, embarrassment.

Or *Two*, stand still.
                              You were not advising—
No sign of distress, no pause or look,
Just a constant slap at the gorgeous face
Consuming you. Two safe yachts passed
In practical reach; you asked them nothing.

So for once myself I stood and offered
Nothing, having offered my life the night
Before and for some years past.
                              You held
Your own through the next few minutes.
I could gauge you against the one visible buoy,
Knobbed with the standard pelican dozing
Near the spot you'd seized in the silent flux—
Expensive, I knew.
                              I held mine.
By then I was on our midget porch—
A squad of poolside lunchers behind;
Palms to left, coral boulders to right
(To form which, billions of sentient lives
Had volunteered bodies less fragile than yours).
You were only a hundred yards away.
Did you see me at all? I waved one time—
A modified Indian-greeting, palm-out,
Inviting an answer.
                              Nothing, I thought.
Did I miss some plea? I waited two minutes,
Monstrous gap.
                   Then you vanished;
Were swept down left past the pelican,
Still afloat but not stroking, arms abandoned.
The next pier hid you.
                              I must have prayed.
But what I remember is combing my hair
And walking at a sane brisk clip out the door
Into sun—past the pool and a girl mock-drowning
A boy who'd seemed all week her brother;
Then into the street past the First Shell Shop

And its grimy display of the Giant Clam,
Threat to Pearl Divers; then on to the pier
Behind which you'd vanished two minutes before.
I thought you were dead. I was calm with the thought.
It filled my skull like a plug of gelid fat,
Room for nothing else.

           At the pier there was
One boat, a forty-foot ancient—*Proud Mari*—
And on it a middle-aged woman in a 1940s
Tank suit, coiling rope. I stopped.
She looked and awarded my wait a grin
Bleak as her timbers. Helpless, I smiled—
The hulk had blanked my view of the water—
And gathered to ask if she'd seen a swimmer
In trouble just now.

         You rose at the far side—
Her port rail, soaked: your hands, head, face.
You didn't see me. You said to the woman
"Can I land here please? I'm a little bushed."
You were ivory, translucent in the final seconds
Of total exhaustion.

         She said "Help yourself"
And went on coiling.

         You managed to haul
Your legs aboard (there were still two, intact).
They bore you the moments you shuddered in glare,
Lovely as anything borne by the earth
That noon—any noon—and *seen*
By me in lucid perfection of love
That moment, though I'd watched you drown.

         Then you strode
Forward, frail as a calf on your pins,
And were over the near side and six feet away
Before you saw me, your disyllabic "Hi"
Preserved in its brightness and plunging distance.
You might well have asked "What are you here for?"—
I needed proof you were really alive—
But you said "Lunch time"

         And I said "True."

It was true; we ate it by the pool—shrimp
Salad and a butterscotch pie so rich
I expected a carbohydrate fit any instant.
It never struck and when (over coffee)
You lightly sketched your recent dilemma,
I concealed my witness, listened rapt,
And expressed post-facto restrained delight
At your narrow luck.
                 My full delight
Poured freely after dark when, stronger, you rose
On cool sheets above me and rode through
Twelve long minutes of danger toward another
Wordless rescue, borne by me
(The next word was *Thanks*, conceded by both).

I was also asking pardon in every cell,
And I felt you give it from an endless horde.
But I never spoke my offer again—
Simply my life—and never confessed
That paralyzed witness of your capture by the sea,
Its release or abandonment of what it had left you.

What had it left you? Tell me
That please. What have we left you?

Telling you now, I find what's left
In my own swept head—my silent knowledge
As you vanished in cedars years ago:
I required your life.
                 The offer stands.

TWO

NINE MYSTERIES

(Four Joyful, Four Sorrowful, One Glorious)

The Angel Gabriel was sent from God to a city in Galilee named Nazareth to a virgin promised to a man named Joseph of the house of David. The virgin's name was Mary. Coming in on her he said "Rejoice, beloved! The Lord is with you." LUKE 1: 26–28

ANNUNCIATION

The angel tries to imagine *need*.
Till now he has not stood near a girl—
Odd generals, magistrates, prophets in skins—
And since his mission is to cry "Beloved!"
And warn of the coming down on her
Of absolute need, he pauses to study
Her opaque hands—both open toward him
And strains to know what need could draw
The Heart of Light to settle on this
Dun child, clay-brown, when curved space
Burns with willing vessels compounded of air.
He feels he is failing; is balked by skin,
Hair, eyes dense as coal.
"Beloved" clogs his throat. He blinks.
Nothing needs this. He has misunderstood.

The girl though has passed through shock to honor
And begins to smile. She plans to speak.
Her dry lips part. *"Me."* She nods.

The low room fills that instant with dark
Which is also wind—a room not two
Of her short steps wide, plugged with dark
(Outside it is three, March afternoon).
In the cube, black as a cold star's core,
One small point shines—her lean face
Licked by a joy no seraph has shown,
An ardor of need held back for this
And bound to kill.
                    But slowly she dims,
The room recovers, she opens a fist.

The angel can speak. "Rejoice, beloved!"

The girl laughs one high note, polite—
Cold news—then kneels by her cot to thank him.

37

Now the birth of Jesus Messiah was like this. When his mother Mary was promised to Joseph before they came together she was found big-bellied by the Holy Spirit.

Now Joseph her husband being good and not wanting to disgrace her decided secretly to dismiss her.

But while he considered these things—look—an angel of the Lord appeared to him in a dream saying "Joseph son of David, don't fear to accept Mary your wife since the thing fathered in her is from the Holy Spirit." MATTHEW 1: 18–20

REPARATION

I'm not especially known for dreams—
There is one though that has had some fame
In which the angel visits me, sleeping,
And says I'm to marry the girl anyhow;
That her story is true.
     The dream was true—
I had it, I mean: angel-visit and explanation,
That I choose to believe as far as it went.
What is not so famous (entirely secret
Till now in fact) is a second dream
That, the more I think, I think came first.

We were in a room—her mother's house—
In natural light, some distance apart.
Her mother had left us a moment before,
And we were alone for the first time really—
(I'd watched her alone at the well, in her garden;
But always till now in open space,
No walls round us).
     Our arms were down
But our eyes met closely. I knew two things—
That her body, small for her age though sturdy,
Was an adequate hive for making the boy
I'd failed to make on my late dry wife;
That I'd fail again. I wondered *why?*
There was ample evidence my body worked—
Ducked and nodded at appropriate sights—

But no cause dawned: just desolate news
That nothing would come of this, not from me.
I didn't move. I said "Is it true?"
She said a plain "No" and made one move—
One step that consumed the space between us,
One hand to raise my cold right wrist
And spread my palm, one finger pressed
In the palm, then gone.
                  Alone in the room
I watched what I had—the hand, broad hand
That had howled, blank *howled,* for a thing to hold.

I was given two things. The spot she'd touched
Blistered and burst; a brown stem rose
And ramified slowly in tiers of thorns—
Desert shrub. Then beneath the shrub
A child condensed, size of the second
Joint of my thumb, with a manchild's organs—
Perfect, the size of three barley grains:
The thing I'd get. So I shut my hand
Upon it gently and have lived with that.

The more I've thought, the more that seems
My only dream—untold till now,
As I said; now told. My hand has adequately
Held it till now.
              Look here. Still mine.

She bore her firstborn son and wrapped him and laid him in a man-
ger since there was no room for them in the inn.   LUKE 2: 7

CHRIST CHILD'S SONG AT THE
END OF THE NIGHT

I have, to be sure, enjoyed the event
And am conscious of various efforts involved—
Trips by ass, foot, camel,
Wing—to welcome what must necessarily
Seem a bafflement (a normal
Boy, ten fingers and toes, brown eyes
And hair) at the narrow end
Of angel prophecies, celestial consorts,
Stellar anomalies, perturbations.

None seemed perturbed. All grinned and bowed;
All left some token of satisfaction—
Free-will offerings in lieu of tickets
To the single display that will not recur.

Now in late quiet, my parents
Asleep, I'm free to think the last
Free thought I'll be allowed. Let it stand,
Grateful chord to the evening's music—
Grateful, short, unavoidably true—

Though handsomely asked, every other one here
Could have stayed at home—Joseph, my mother,
Could still be single in Nazareth: barren.
Shepherds and magi consented with near-
Unseemly ease. Angels themselves were
Free to choose—note the famous
Dissenter, hid there by the door.
I am the one in the reach
Of time who is given no choice,
The chosen child.

They came to the house of the synagogue leader. Jesus saw a commotion, people weeping and wailing hard. Entering he said to them "Why make a commotion and weep? The child is not dead but sleeps."

They mocked him.

But expelling them all he took the child's father, mother and those with him and went in where the child was. Grasping the child's hand he said to her "Talitha koum" which is translated "Little girl, I tell you rise."

At once the little girl stood and walked round—she was twelve years old—and at once they were astonished with great wildness.

MARK 5: 38–42

DEAD GIRL

I have died and am glad.
My body is twelve years old on my bed.
I can see it there and the room around it,
The hall outside, all the people I knew.
I am smaller than I thought—they are pressing me down
Like a bale with their eyes; and my father has brought in
Two old men with flutes, four expensive wailers
Who must be boys but look like dolls.
I am shrinking from that (I mainly loved music)
Or was shrinking when I died. I remember clearly.
My father kept asking if I was in pain;
And I nodded Yes, though I'd gone past pain.
Pain had passed on some good while before
When it dawned on me *No one will touch me.*
Once I died they would wash me and bind me tight.
Then no one would ever touch me again—
I would be unclean; men would walk
Whole miles not to touch my tomb (our family
Has a tomb: I will be on a slab in the dark tomorrow).
I was thinking that and may have been smiling,
So calm anyhow that the way I knew
I had finally died was having the bracelet
Cool on my wrist. I was standing outdoors
In light houseclothes and had on my arm

The big dark bracelet that had been Grandmother's
And would come to me on my wedding day—
Worked with monsters' heads and fiery leaves.
I was thoroughly glad and rubbed at the bronze
And smelled my finger and walked on forward
Past the well I would never drink water from again
Toward the edge of a lake.
       There is no one but me.
The dead world is empty and was made for me.
I will never be fed, talked to or touched.
I am glad, as I said, and have left them my body.
It is what they have waited twelve years to get.
I sit on the wet rocks and watch them have it
With their eyes—bats feeding—
Till almost dark. I am cool and calm.
I have seen a single star and thanked it.
They will wail all night.
       But the dead need rest.
When night is thoroughly down, I am tired.
I find a beached dry boat and enter.
I lie on a rag sail and press
My bracelet in on a chest where no
Heart beats, cold against me
(I have still not warmed it; I never will).
Then I shut my eyes and shut out all—
Stars, lake, that room, my twelve-year-old
Body bled by grief of men
Who needed me; will now never touch me.
I make one strong thrust out with my mind
And float on a rest I smile to meet—
Black water beneath me that bears my weight,
Alone in my wedding-ware for good.

This sleep will last till the end of things.

They got their hands on Jesus and seized him.

But one of the bystanders drawing a sword struck the high priest's slave and cut off his ear.

Speaking out Jesus said to them "Did you come out with swords and sticks as if against a rebel to arrest me? Daily I was with you in the Temple teaching and you didn't seize me. But the scriptures must be done."

Deserting him they all ran.

One young man followed him dressed in a linen shirt over his naked body. They seized him but leaving the shirt behind he fled naked.

Then they took Jesus off to the high priest and all the chief priests, elders and scholars gathered.   MARK 14: 46–53

NAKED BOY

He got to our house at ten that morning,
Alone, not hungry—first time
I'd seen him completely alone. The mob
That had trailed him all week—all year—
Was simply gone. He'd hid from them somehow
And turned up here—himself, no disguise:
Not even the famous adhesive woman
In sight or John. My mother and Rhoda
Had left a little before since shops
Would mostly close at noon, so I
Met him in the porch and said she was gone.
He nodded—"I came to help you."
I couldn't think how but my pleasure
Must have looked like bewilderment. He said
"The hen house." I remembered telling him
That Mother had asked me to build a coop,
That I'd gathered boards and would get to it soon.
But I hadn't meant this day—Passover
Ban began at noon, no work after noon.
I said "We'd never get it finished by noon."
He said "We'll finish." I'd have seized adders
For him, so I just led him out
To the yard; and with hens limping round us,

He carefully showed me how to start;
Then sat on a ledge to watch me at it,
Coming over occasionally to do something right.

I worked in a steady fever of joy,
Assuming and fearing he'd leave any minute
Or the friends would find him. He never
Went farther than three steps from me, and nobody
Came but Mother and Rhoda just before
Noon with all they'd bought
For the long weekend. He only told Mother
"I'm here to help him. We'll work till it's done."
She thanked him but said we should come in
At noon. He just said "We'll finish,"
And we worked right through the volley of horns
From Temple Hill announcing ban.
By the time we had got the job on its feet,
It was three o'clock; and nothing was left
But the hard part—the door, fitting
The door. He took over then and started
On that; but to keep me busy, he said
"Please tell me all your life."
I laughed but he said "No, please" so I did.
He listened as if my thin news
Was one last missing rail
For some bigger hut he had
In mind, though all I could tell was the trifling
Schedule of fifteen years in my father's
House, my father's death three months
Before.
          I'd got to that end when the twelve
Friends shuffled up by twos and threes
From whatever day they'd had without him.
I understood then that they'd known
Where he was and had kept their distance, which proved
More than ever he'd chosen the time
With me. They lay round the yard while
He hung the door, and Mother came out
And whispered to me to go to my uncle's

Downhill for seder—he'd asked to eat
Here with his friends, and her hands were full.
I said out loud "I'll stay close
And help." He heard me, faced me,
Shook his head once No. Then he set down
The knife he was trimming the door with,
Turned (no look back) and climbed
Eight steps to our high room,
Friends behind him.
           So I stayed
To finish the door he'd abandoned,
Put one scared hen in to give her
A lead, then ignored Rhoda's call
To wash for my uncle's and decided to walk
Out past Hinom to a cut in rock
Where I lie when I'm low and complain to bushes,
The odd lost goat or lunatic.
           But the streets
Were solid with gentiles, soldiers and a few
Northern hicks who were in town
For more than lamb with herbs; and after
A few yards of bucking crowds—relays
Of hands plucking at me in dark till they came
To seem the promise I needed:
That the secret heart of town was tender,
Had reached for me and would fold me in
If I nodded or smiled—I bared my
Excellent teeth to the dry air
And grinned through a slow wide wheel
Round Zion.
           No taker. I was all
One piece, back at Mother's—safe,
Entirely me. Caged, prowling in my bones,
And as likely to sleep as a tom in a ring
Of staring dogs.
           But I climbed to my own
Room and, stripped on my mat, gave myself
To myself—not quite a cold supper, a meal
Nonetheless: short, soporific.

*

Mother touched me later—I'd dressed before sleep
In a clean nightshirt—and said, all dark,
"Quick. To the garden. Lead him here
Fast." She left as quickly.
                                        I lay still,
Understanding clearly—*Butchery, or the dream
Of butchery, begins.* I did not plan to move.
I planned to sleep and did; then dreamed
That my father had not died but, cured, sat
With Mother as I came down at dawn for food
And said "I have waited all night for you."

So I woke, sick with shame, and ran in my shirt
Through ways only slightly less packed than before—
Past three distinct voices requesting me—down and cross
Kidron, uphill to the garden.
                                        They already had
Him (no sign of the others except for
Redhead, back on the rim of torchlight,
Explaining). A Temple guard held Jesus
By the elbows. I doubt he saw me, but he looked
My way very steadily.
                                        So I went on toward him
And nobody stopped me. His gaze never broke—
No recognition, no warning—but when
I was three steps short of his face,
He said "Would the hens go into the house?"
I said "Yes." Then he said he was sorry.
I understood he didn't mean the hens;
But before I could ask "For what?" or forgive him,
The guard grabbed my shoulder with far more strength
Than he held Jesus with.
                                        I stood a long moment,
Wrenched back hard. He held onto Jesus
But struggled with me enough to tear my shirt.
Then Jesus said "*Leave.*" I tore clean free,
Stood another instant naked. The guard
Called for help, but by then I was dark.

*

It had been a repeated dread of course—
Stripped in the streets, no cover near—
But nobody bothered following; and I ran
Through deeper black toward the edge of houses,
Then walked to my moaning place in the rock
And managed sleep—dreamless, cold.

When I woke, brown day was seeping up.
I stood, brushed grit from my side
And face and walked to my mother—bare
As she'd borne me, through streets as bare. I didn't
Think of him till, in sight of our gate,
A voice in a window—the one wake soul—
Said "You. Now. Please."
                              I looked
And my mind stalled; but I never stalled,
Though a hand reached toward me—cupped and clean.
I strode in my cold skin the last steps home,
My dazzling hide.

Now when Pilate was sitting on the judgment bench his wife sent to him saying "Do nothing to that good man for I suffered much today in a dream because of him." MATTHEW 27: 19

SLEEPING WIFE

We'd heard weird news all winter,
Filtered south—dead walking, wounds
Sealing—but I'd seen him just once
The previous morning as we crossed the Court
Of the Gentiles, bound for our Residence flat.
He lectured a modest huddle of rural
Pickers and scratchers (none visibly
Cured) and stood, arms up,
Spoon-thumbs, back to me—which helps
Explain his showing in the dream: younger,
Leaner, some distance from a man.

It was already light. My husband had
Left. I dozed, postponing the annual
Lamb-slaughter pending at our window.
                                        He stood
In the door—black hair to his shoulders,
Stray wires on his chin: calm as wax.
I knew it was him when I called his name—
He'd made no noise, never did; the cries
Were mine. How I put that name to that
Face is still odd. Once named he could
Move. I was trusting he'd grin; but
The face rushed on, iron arrow. At
The bed he drew off the sheet, bowed my
Legs, bent, entered. Understand—no
Man's slim thrust, a child's clawing:
Dry fingers, arms, head,
Chest, hips, legs, feet.
I mentioned cries—*screams* (no help
Heard or came)—but I never objected;
And in maybe five minutes he'd packed me
Entirely with his crawl, fork to crown,

And rested at the absolute walls of my skin
So I only sucked spoonsful of air,
Bird-sips. I'd never breathe
Deep till I bore him somehow.

I woke, sent word (not detailing the dream);
And failed as has been fairly customary.
Our only child strangled inside me
Fourteen years ago—male, I was told.

Mary the Magdalene turned and saw Jesus standing, not that she knew it was Jesus.

Jesus said to her "Woman, why cry? Whom do you want?"

She thinking it was the gardener said to him "Sir, if you carried him off tell me where you put him and I'll take him."

Jesus said to her "Mary."

Turning she said to him in Hebrew "Rabboni" which means Teacher.

Jesus said to her "Don't touch me for I haven't yet gone up to the Father. But go to my brothers and tell them 'I'm going up to my Father and your Father, my God and your God.' " JOHN 20: 14–17

RESURRECTION

She's come a last time before day to touch him.
Last and first. Till now she has not—
Though till him what she'd known
Was ways to touch, valuable ways
That got her her life: small life
Promising to end, early rest.
Friday they'd only had time to loop him
In myrrh and aloes with linen strips
When Sabbath stopped them.
                           She's filled thirty hours
With hope of this, a private end—
Five minutes alone at the instant of day
To find his face and feet, wash them.
Then the gang of others, parceling him
(She'd hid all Saturday to plan in secret,
To come here unfollowed in Sunday dark).
She even knows her way round guards,
Her way to move rock—her old way, her—
And have her chance and be gone by light
To whatever house will feed her now.

No guard, no rock. Her fast hands
Scratch at the small thick dark. No body
On the ledge—blank yards of linen, stiff

With blood.
   Late, she thinks. She says "*Again*."
All her life she has missed her needs
By moments. Simple needs.
     She shudders as demons
Pluck at her face—blind cocks, horn beaks
That will gouge till they find old holes
In. They touch her at least, know her slick skin.
She half-grins in welcome, slumps on the ledge.
Hot padding. She gnaws it.
     What she does not know—
Outside it is day. In the garden he hunts
Her, her first. He is stunned—
Calf, wet colt, boy dredged from sleep.
Each step toward her, he burns with fresh blood
Rushing his legs. He feels he has won
All he swore to win, can face her now.

When she steps from the grave, sees him, knows,
He will not let her touch him.

Throwing the coins down in the Temple Judas left and going off
hanged himself.   MATTHEW 27: 5

INSTRUCTION

I'm given the time it takes to tell you
Precisely this. Ask no questions.
There was one sighting which
Has not been reported by loyalists.
Peter, John, Mary, James
Have milked tears enough with their
Reunions to farm a fair-sized
Salt-lick in Sodom. I don't grudge them
That. The one not reported however
Was to me.
         I'd got out of town by Friday
Dawn to miss the dustup I launched
In the garden. The cash was slung in my left
Groin, nudging other privates,
For the seven-mile walk to Emmaus—
The inn. We'd never worked that.
I could sleep the hours it would take to kosher
Him white as veal, the loyalists to note they'd
Failed him equally and scuttle home—
Dried boats, nets, wives,
Mothers-in-law. Then I'd head back
To town for the sinecure they'd thrown in
To sweeten the cash—bookkeeper
At the licensed Temple lamb-and-dove
Purveyance: no one cracked a smile.
I'd start Monday morning, under light
Guard till Friday (they had a week's
Worth of anxiety for me; I'd
Known the eleven through a year on the road
And knew I was safe—they'd growl but
On fast feet: Parthian growls).
               I slept
Two days, waking only to think I'd
Never slept better and gnaw

A flat cake I'd hooked on the way
And ask if the rest—alluvial mud—
Wasn't better reward than cash or job
Or memory of Peter's white face
In fireshine, slick with fright:
Blown hog's bladder burst
By boys (the answer was Yes and I'd sleep
Again).
              Sunday evening I was sated but
Hungry. I skimmed my eyes with cool
Dry fingers, rehung the privates
And went down to eat in the common room—
Loud clutch of Passover pilgrims
Bound north, no face I knew.
I'd finished when another three entered
And sat—Klopas, his squat wife, a trim
Tan stranger. The Klopases had bankrolled
Us, steady but stingy, through Galilee.
My legs jerked to leave, then locked me
In. I was legal; I'd make my first
Stand here. But they talked to the stranger
And never looked up. I licked at
My bowl and filled my space—paid-up patron.
The window over them faced due-
West, so I fixed on that and bathed
In sunset.
              The girl brought their food.
They groveled to bless it. The stranger stood,
Neat as a sprout sucked up in a morning.
It was him, no question—crammed-
Down, a little ashy at the gills but
Pleasant and coming toward me.
I tried again to rise in the days
It took him to reach my bench;
Legs refused.
              His hands were ruined—
Brown holes, barely dry—
But otherwise fit. I begged not to touch
Them, though I didn't speak.

He kept silent too,
Kept hands at his thighs.
No pause or stare, the smile
Never quit. He bent
To my hair and pressed it once, quite lengthily,
With a mouth that seemed his usual mouth—
No stars or rays, no sizzling brand—
Then walked the breadth of the floor and out.
I had not had to touch him—
Not direct, not skin.
I waited for roars, leaps, laughs
From the room. Klopas and his wife were chewing
In tears, drowned in the gift.
No one else had looked.
I sat till the next gnat
Sapped my heel, then stood as I was—
Freed to stand into honor like rain—
And went through the same door,
Same empty yard.
    Halfway back
To town in dark dry as meal, I
Groped out a tree that promised to hold.
Honor had lasted a full three miles.
I lasted a full two minutes
By the neck, longer than planned—my well-oiled belt
(The privates were insufficient ballast).
Nobody claimed body or ballast;
We two were the bachelors.
     You may now ask questions.

Saying these things—with them looking—Jesus was lifted up and a cloud took him from their eyes.   ACTS 1: 9

ASCENSION

I expected one question the moment I was back—
Where did you go? Nobody asked it.
In thirty-nine days of astounding them
At our various haunts from Jerusalem
To the Sea and demonstrating my obvious
Self—tangible as a good plow
And roughly as worn—I heard only
One thing in several forms:
Who are you? I continued to show them
The answer was plain—*I'm what I've been
From the start. Feel me.* Some were readier
Than others to accept—Magdalene, Thomas:
She grabbing, he gouging.
Some came forward scared as boys
That have turned up a snake in a gully,
Sleep or dead—Andrew, young Mark.
Some never came at all—my brother James,
Which was no great surprise; Levi and John.
I kept on thinking John was the hold-out—
Beloved John—that when he got his
Nerve up, felt me once more,
Proved to us both I was *me* but *leaving,*
Then I could leave.
            I'd prepared my speech.
John would step up and kiss my left
Cheek-bone (thereby canceling
Judas' last greeting, damp still
And cool though spring days blew past it,
Helpless to warm); then would step
Back and nod acceptance of change—
You, departing. Then I would say
*In the thirty-nine hours when death
Begins, you do not sleep. You rest
And recall every living person*

You loved and expected. The rest comes in this—
You no longer expect them: no more
Than horses eating in ditches expect
Other horses. You think "That was it.
Thirty years to learn that." Then you
Wake and are happy. I even tracked
Him down on a fishing trip; but he kept
Safe distance between us, two steps.
And I knew I shouldn't force him.

                         So the fortieth
Day I resigned myself to a longer
Wait. We were back in Jerusalem—over in
The celebrated terrible garden, just olive
Blooms now. Ten of the pupils were
Sitting with me, discussing escape—
I was hunted of course and was well-
Disguised as a touring Greek.
John was in town, tending my mother
Who was ailing slightly or so
We'd heard: I still hadn't seen her,
Avoiding evidence of my worst
Harm.

        But here they came. Peter
Saw them first, at the foot of the hill,
And whispered to me. There was time
To leave. I'd have been overhill
In Bethany by the time they
Arrived if I'd left then, but
I held my ground—for John not
Her.

       It should have been for her.
I sat in dread, hard as I'd known
Here the night they seized me, and let
Her come.

              She was ruined as the town itself
Would be—sewn with salt, barren
By me: barely fifty, stunned
As eighty. Or so it looked at nearing
Range; but she walked on her own and hurried

A little the last few yards,
Stopping an instant three steps
From me; then coming the whole way,
Kissing my left cheek, taking my
Right hand and touching her finger
To the rosy scar. Then she laid the whole
Palm over her mouth, returned it
To me and said *"Promise me*
It is possible to bear."
                          I thought she meant
Me, for her to bear the rest
Of me. I doubted I could promise that
Honestly.
            But she said *"Leaving."*
I could promise that, having undergone
Considerable pain to leave and return—
And answer this question, finally asked.
I could answer it. I laughed and nodded—
She could halfway smile—and found I was free
To leave, and left.

THREE

PICTURES OF THE DEAD

1. ROBERT FROST, 1951

Begin then, Sisters of the sacred well—
"Most beautiful line the world affords,
And it can be *learned*," you say and repeat
It three slow times in your world-
Famed curmudgeon growl.
                        I'm
Eighteen, silent in a team of Chapel
Hill Ph.D.'s all
Pumping for inside dope on Ezra
Pound. You're seventy-seven, refusing,
Substituting Milton and making us
Take it—for the hour at least, all
You'll give.
              On the spot, I
Take it for no better reason than
Your frightening face, beat of your elephant
Hide on pine, unanswerable voice.
I was right. Still am, still
Learning the line.

2. W. H. AUDEN, 1957

We're dining alone at The Bear in Woodstock.
You've drunk your regulation two gins-and-
French, then insisted on buying the wine—
Lafite. I remember no other word you
Said nor what we ate in the packed
Small room (I'm to pay for the food);
Only that after in late spring
Evening, you seem to see nothing
As I drive us through Blenheim Park: still
Earth's clear apex for me.
                              Back at my
Rooms in mean brick Headington—
A few yards down from mean
Tolkien, secreting his dream—I produce
A friend's gift from a Christmas
Nervous collapse in Madeira: hand-
Lettered 1930 Madeira,
Year of your *Poems*. You seem not
To notice; say only as you taste
"It's turned to gin." You sit in my chair,
I at your knees on the leatherette
Hassock. We drink all the gin.
I remember we laughed but again
No word of all we said; only that
At one unheralded moment, mid-sentence,
You lean with the grace of an oak umbrella-
Rack, kiss me twice rapid-fire
On the dry right cheek.
They remain—and my thanks.

3. ROBERT LOWELL, 1968

The night you died in a New York cab,
Here in my bed (oblivious) I dreamt
We were on my terrace again—you,
Jack Knowles, Charlie Smith and
I.
   We eat my leftover
Curry and rice, lie back to laugh
In April sun under baby leaves
While you read us Auden's "On the Circuit"—
I shift so frequently, so fast,
I cannot now say where I was
The evening before last,
Unless some singular event
Should intervene to save the place,
A truly asinine remark,
A soul-bewitching face.
The place (recent scene of a love
Entertaining as the Dresden fire-storm)
Is saved again by your broad mug—
Half-Homeric, half-mad,
Burnt over by intermittent winds
That will get you yet. Still the dream is
Happy and oddly actual, mere
Memory.
        I wake refreshed,
Do a good morning's work,
Drive in for mail, then on to the shop
To buy your new *Selected Poems.*
As I pay, the clerk says "Too
Young to die"—the news on you.
Home I tell the maid my dream
And how you died while it came.
She says "That was nothing but his
Spirit as it left, passing through places
It had been happy in."
          You were
Welcome both times.

ARCHAIC TORSO OF APOLLO

Look. You'll never conceive his head.
Eyes blank as apples ripen to this day
Under Greek junk, were crushed to lime for mortar.
But here the body burns, amends for blindness.
Legs, arms, thrust down—torches for his dark.

So he blinds you. So his smile survives
In wings of muscle lifting from his sex.
Permit his shining. Otherwise he'll hulk,
Another mineral bore cooling his heels.

Wait. If not he'll never break his chains
And stalk—now!—one step crams the room with light.
A star swells madly, famished for what fuel?
You. His chest, legs, haunches, sex—now eyes.
All locked on you. Change your life.

after Rilke

FOUND, FOR MY BROTHER

Here in my dream of Uncle Grant's shack,
Grubbing (for what?) in the packed fawn
Clay—alone, no human or bird to watch—
I find your old red square sand-shovel.
Neither of us can have seen it for thirty-odd years;
And surely it has either dissolved where you lost it
Or survived reforging for an interim war
(Dissolute atoms in the schist of Korea;
The thickets southward, your Vietnam).
It had leached anyhow from my consciousness.
I've longed occasionally for toys of my own—
The Seven-Dwarf set of castile soap,
The pillbox of dried mud from Hitler's Mercedes,
The boy-sized Charlie McCarthy with hinged lips—
But hardly for yours. Yours were weapons—
A footlocker-armory of realistic guns:
Colts, Lugers, Flash Gordons;
And you miles gentler than the Dalai Lama,
Despite your party renditions, age four,
Of "Don't Fence Me In!" with cap-
Pistol chorus (piano by me)—
Yet here my hands uncover this peaceful
Implement, realistic and real. I stroke it,
Quick to recall; then reinter it,
Certain it will constitute treasure for you—
Another true self endured and found.

Awake, tomorrow, I bring you here—
Actual site (the house long gone)—
We crouch by the oak, my fingers hunt
Unerringly.
                You own it again.

TO MY NIECE—OUR PHOTOGRAPH
IN A HAMMOCK

No one thinks you are mine.
I could have bought you from gypsies
Or—desperate, if solitude had left me desperate—
From a defrocked doctor who bootlegs at night,
With abortions and morphine, a sideline of babies:
Derelict blond blue-eyed bastard
In my Black-Welsh arms.

They're wrong. You are.
At eighteen months—a day, a moment—
You are my remains, my physical remains;
And you hoard already, little banker (no choice),
Every egg you will ever pay out on speculation,
Four hundred maybe in your fertile years.
Each one, of thousands—you're chocked for safety;
Roed like a shad against loneliness, extinction—
Guards already in final form, unknown as your death,
Some of the instructions I might have passed to Man.

Man may yet do without them.
If our picture is omen, you may seal your vaults,
Say the monthly No to the monthly hope,
Balk every try at blind continuance;
For though, in the frame, my hands strain to hold you,
You struggle to escape—me, your volunteering life
That swells each instant in you, presses every wall—
And you laugh, not with me but elsewhere, outward.
I know in retrospect that you laugh at the sky
Northwest of my roof, but what decked the sky
For you that day?—that evening, evening light.
What vision? What clear shaft opening to joy?
Like a white baby-seal—a dugong calf!—
You paddle the June air around us toward freedom.

*

I am laughing for the cameraman (your laughing father)
So I do not notice and wouldn't mind.
Here, I have you safely—my arms vs. yours—
And if, in years, your struggles wrench you loose,
Award you solitude, sterility, space,
The world will return you in hunger or duty
(It has brought me to you; I am choosing to hold you);
Trap you, raving, gnashing: feed you its diet.

Look. Neither of us noticed the news of that day—
You rapt in babyhood, I in pleasure—
The bedrock above which we hung and giggled.
Our picture, pitiless monitor, preserves it:
Even the hammock we swing in is a net.

I SAY OF ANY MAN

I say of any man, when he is good
   And wise, what does he need? Will some things
      Feed his soul? Is there an ear of corn,
         A secret vineyard ripening in the earth

To nourish him? Here is the truth of that—
   A friend may be the loved one, art is
      Much. Dear friend, here is the truth of you—
         Daedalus' ghost is yours, the summer woods'.

after **Hölderlin**

AURORA

Is it unacceptably
Self-absorbed
To ask if tonight's
Colossal veil
Of ascendant light
In the boreal sky
(First aurora
Visible to me
And displayed precisely
Twenty-four hours
Beyond the line
We drew beneath
Two perfect days)
Is admonition,
Responsive glory,
Or ions stunned
In our conjunction
And fleeing north?
The record can
At least confirm
That colors shifted
Steadily through
The ten cold minutes
I stood to watch,
Faced opposite your south—
No two alike,
All tinctures of blood.

A RAINBOW AND A DAY-OLD CALF

Four months of straining
To burn each other to the ground,
Strew the ashes; and here we agree
To a sunset walk in the greening field—
Day after April Fool, dry breeze—and
Are met by a rainbow in shameless stride
And a day-old calf who thinks it's hid
In two strands of honeysuckle,
Plain as a blaze.
                    I note the single omen
They make—arc and hider—
Read it for hope.

MAN AND FAUN

MAN   This narrow stream pours to a waterfall;
        And—what is that, a hairy shank which hangs
        From dark moss cushioned onto dripping rocks?
        The thicket of its head mats round a horn.
        In my long hunting—woods, distant hills—
        I have not yet seen this: no, do not move!
        I bar all paths, shelter. Stand, face me.
        Calming ripples lap a split goat's hoof.

FAUN   We neither will be glad you found me here.

MAN   I knew of beasts like you from ancient books,
        Not that such useless things survived, ran free.

FAUN   When—as you will—you drive me to depart,
        Starved you'll thrash your woods for worthy prey—
        Your only plunder: rodents, blind worms, slugs—
        And when you've hacked your path through every thorn,
        All your wells will dry into the sand.

MAN   Warn me, huddled freak?—I who have killed
        Giants, hydras, gorgons, glimpsed the basilisk;
        Cleared wilderness, forced wilderness to yield?
        Where black swamps smoked, grain ripens in the light;
        Cattle safely pasture my green hills,
        Farms flourish, cities rise, gardens gleam,
        And woods enough survive for stag and doe.
        My treasures I have dredged from sea and earth—
        Stones themselves concede my victory;
        Light and order strengthen in my tracks.
        State your purpose, relic of chaos.

FAUN   You are one man and where your vision fails,
        My eyes burn on. You recognize no brink
        Till you plunge to its pit—broken, torn.
        When your grain ripens, when your cattle thrive,
        When trees bend to you with their oil and grapes,
        You call these recompense for labor, craft.
        But earths that breathed beneath this crust still breathe,

        Have never died, are welded in a chain
        That will flail mad the hour one link is breached.
        This was the day allotted for your rule.
        Now surrender—you have seen the faun.
        Doom begins. The cunning able mind,
        Your light and guide, softens as you stand.
        Your bond with beast and dirt also dissolves.
        Revulsion, lust, tumult, monotony,
        Dust and flare and death and origin—
        Your grip upon the buried chain is broke.

MAN   Who told you this? Gods provide for me.

FAUN   Gods have their day like men. You were, you died,
        And never knew your secret name.

MAN   Blank raving!

FAUN   Fall and pray to me that blankly raves.

MAN   Bitter monster—twisted spine and mouth—
        I see in you, ruined mirror, my old face.
        In pity I delay my fatal spear.

FAUN   No beast knows shame; no man knows gratitude.
        All your craft, and you have never learned
        The precious thing. Yet I have dumbly served.
        Hear final warning—kill me, kill yourself.
        Where my fur brushed, milk gathered, warm milk gushed.
        Where my hoof did not press, no stalk saw light.
        Were your mind all you'd had—ages since,
        Your kind, your hectic business had stopped;
        Woods had blackened, seedbeds burned to ash.
        I was the water at the roots of life.

after Stefan George

TOWN CREEK

Two hours from home
(My home), we climb a mound
Heaped *circa* 1480 by the Creeks—
Tidily refurbished for the grade schools,
Idle adults scouting savagery.

On top, a box mud temple
To the god—sole faithful Sun.
Inside, pole benches—one a vacant altar.
Straw roof, pierced by a smoke hole, still transmits
His daily visit to the dugout hearth.

We edge into an unrequited glare;
You lean to touch the fuel
(Four pine logs). None here but us,
Five hundred years too late.

Whoever else embraced by this dead fire?

DIVINE PROPOSITIONS

That the animals love us.
That horses the size of granite bluffs
Will lay their huge hearts beside us
At night and sleep till we wake.
That wolves who gnash down stags in air
Will nurse our lost young,
Return them whole.

That you have laid your hawk head here
In my room (strange as the ocean floor),
Borne twenty nights' danger,
Returned each dusk.

YOUR ELEMENT

Earth, Air, Water, Fire—
The four meet in you
But your element is Silence,
The hard clear ether in which
You advance—

As last night,
Scraping dishes alone,
I caught at the window
A wash of lights,
The car they guided,
Your silent upright body
Through leaves,
Bent against me
The whole cool night:
A speechless shield.

BLACK WATER

Black water runs
Down in that ditch.
My love for you
Has locked my tongue.

But you talk love,
Talk loyalty.
A lie grates under
Every word.

So if I speak
My love ten times
And you still lie,
I'll go for good.

I thank you for
The time we had
And wish you luck
In days ahead.

after a German folksong

MEMORANDA

TOWARD JUNCTION

No map can show how—through the world—
Ample in power, clean in aim,
You move toward me. Incredibly, you do.
Certain the route is no print-out
From an odds machine, I wonder *Who?*
Some one or thing is sending you.
I suspect an intercession, a dead
But potent witness who has caught a burst
Of my gentlemanly thirty-year-long
Bellow and throws the switches that shunt
You here. Candidates narrow
To my mother or father, a bachelor cousin,
And Wystan Auden—not because he's starred
On James Merrill's Ouija or because
I'm reading the new biography he'd rightly
Have loathed (obtuse as a mirror) but because,
Despite his cold-douche kindness,
He's the one of the numerous familiar
Dead who'd have sought the post:
Yard-master of lines for lives he'd touched.
See him at the console, straining at lights
(All green for him), ears peeled
For groans, beaming again and sure
For once he can meet the task.
                              You're
Not here yet. Proceed respectfully,
Observe timetables, augment the prayer:
Wystan—whoever, whatever—clear
The rails.

MEMORANDUM 1

At the first revelation of your body in the room—
Shabby dark of a family motel,
Ocean beside us (your first sight of it:
You asked "Will it keep on all through our sleep?"),
My eyes averted to grant you air
You did not require—
You called my name, compelling my look;
And though the body was calm, unflaunted,
Its ample secret flared, your gift,
And you said "None of my clothes are good enough for this."

May never be.

MEMORANDUM 2

You asked him to bless the cross you'd picked
From his narrow room of featherweight rosaries,
Saints' lives bound in frogskin vinyl.
He could no longer stand, and he'd welcomed us in whispers—
"Fifty years here but I come from Tipperary."
He found in his lap the frayed magic band,
Slowly hung it round his neck,
And for maybe a minute whispered to your cross
As he stroked its cellophane wrapper with earnest crosses
Secreted by his own wide hand.
Then from the shelf eight inches to his left,
He took an old eyewash-bottle and squeezed
A drop on the wrapper—more whispers, crosses
Till he offered it to you, potent for use.
When he told us the monks would gather in the chapel
"In five minutes now to sing for ten minutes,"
I asked would he go (we could help him go).
"I've hurt meself. I'll stay here an hour."
His noble skull was glazed cancer-yellow,
His tan hair fallen in saucer clumps,
Only the smile was straining to last.

The blessing undoubtedly endured our night.

MEMORANDUM 3

You are so dark I misapprehend you,
Seizing dry hair when I reach for a hand—
Where are lips, the guarded rims of eyes,
The intact message you promised in daylight?
Mute, you patiently recite yourself;
And slowly I reconstruct you in Braille—
Word of reprieve—then devour you.

No stranger, here or ever, shall read.

MEMORANDUM 4

This famous lake
In its famous hills
Is shut for the winter—
Not a bed to rent,
Canine grouches
In fake-fur
Coats at every dock—
So we stay on wheels
And you reel me past
A sizable gift
In sloped yellow light:
The woods you combed
Ten years ago,
Empty of all but
Your memory now,
A slow hand in them,
Probing for—there—
The ordinary tree
By which (stunned with patience)
You'd wait in hope
Some girl might pop
A strap, flash bare,
You know the last secret.

MEMORANDUM 5

On the nubby teal spread
(Veteran of maybe ten years
Of afternoons silent as this),
You are one compact swagged
Calligraph in phosphorus,
Still but transmitting—
You have earned this
Today. Can you keep it?
I grin my Yes; your eyes take it,
Grave. For the third time
I bolt you down in gobbets—
Strengthening horse-meat,
Rank haunch of bear.

THE FIELD

Isn't this the field where the lodestone is hid?
Hasn't the intact chart to its grave been confided to us?
Aren't we sufficient in breath and limb to walk from here
To the shifting rim of its sovereign draw?
Won't the palms of our bare hands home to the core?
Can't we break inward, hunting, locked but fed?

CUMAEAN SONG

Now last fruit of Cumaean song—
Great wheel of ages, youthful, turns again;
Virgin restored, Saturn's reign restored,
New child sent upon us from high heaven.
Pure Lucina, nod on newborn boy
So with him Iron generations end,
Gold men rise again across the earth,
So your own Apollo reign at last.
    And in your consulate, yours Pollio,
Splendor begins, abundant months proceed—
You guiding, remnants of our wickedness
Be canceled, earth be freed her ancient dread.
    Godly life awaits him. He will see
Heroes ranged with gods, be seen by them;
Will steer a world placated by his father.
    Wandering ivy random with foxglove,
Acanthus smiling mixed with colocasia—
These, Boy, presents poured by untilled earth.
Goats uncalled bring udders bursting milk,
No ox fears lion however huge his power,
Even your cradle blossoms to enfold you,
Serpents perish, perish deadly weeds,
Syrian balsam springs up everywhere.
    Later when you've read heroic glories,
Father's deeds, and know what manhood is,
Slowly plains will gild with waving corn,
Purple grapes droop clustered from wild thorn,
Honeydew distill from hard heart-oak.
Still traces of old fraud will wait in stealth,
Lure men out to try the sea in ships,
Lock towns in walls, divide the earth with plows.
Then again will come a second Tiphys,
Second Argo bearing chosen heroes,
Even war—second war will come,

Hard Achilles sent again to Troy.
   But when strength of time makes man of you,
Merchant seamen will forsake their routes,
Piney ships swap nothing—all be full—
Land not suffer harrow, vine no hook,
Robust plowhand free his team from yoke,
Wool no more learn counterfeiting colors,
Ram himself in pasture change his fleece
Now to blushing purple, now to crocus,
Scarlet ringlets sprout on grazing lambs.
   "Speed the day!" Fates have cried to spindles,
Unison fixed will of destiny.
   Enter—almost time—on your vast honors,
Dear child of gods, strong increment of Jove.
Look—world arcing under heavy dome,
Earth and tracts of sea and heaven's depth.
Look—all jubilate in time at hand.
O last days of long life lengthen for me,
Breath come steady so I tell your deeds;
Neither Thracian Orpheus nor Linus
Ever then could vanquish me in song,
Though one should bring his mother, one his father—
Orpheus, Calliope; Linus, grand Apollo,
Even Pan, if Arcady would judge,
Even Pan would grant my victory.
   Begin, small Boy, to know your mother, smiling—
Ten long months have left her pale and weak.
Begin, small Boy—who does not smile for parents
No god feeds at table, no goddess beds.

after Vergil

FOR LEONTYNE PRICE AFTER ARIADNE

. . . ein Ding wächst
So leicht ins andere. . . .
Wie schaffst du die Verwandlung?
HOFMANNSTHAL

Things easily change to other things
If a goddess speaks—men to trustworthy
Gods, trees to merciful hands.

Find her first. There's only one.
She comes in single relays through time,
Required to live apart in rocks
By water—long nights—surrounding
A solitude deep as her power, its cause
And food.
        There, stand at her door.
Dare her name—*Tall Lioness.*
Beg grace, beg voice. She's forced to yield.

She'll rise unsmiling, speak your hope.
The speech is song. Try to bear it—
Audible light. Eventually
She sings your name. If you last to hear,
The change begins—you're godly then;
Trees bend toward you with loyal love
Till she's still again or memory dies.

It will not die.

THE ANNUAL HERON

December 27th, down for breakfast,
Profoundly fondued from the previous night,
I raise the blinds on panes broadcasting
Cold, a signal—clear sky, sun,
Pond still liquid though thickening
At the rim, and the annual heron
Fifty yards beyond me in rigid profile,
Four feet high, slate gray,
One flat eye, cocked in every cell
(Neck out, legs locked), hunting again:
Fish or me?

His tenth year with me—the fish or me.
I know because when I saw him first,
I wrote him down in my first novel
Which was ending then. He still stands
There, page 169, proffered oasis
For a couple too gorged on mutual
Misery to take his option—consolation *in situ*
Or an emblem of flight, contented self-service.
Hungrier then myself, I wondered;
And now, nine visits later,
Hollow as a whistle, I press this annual
Appearance for a meaning beyond the obvious—
Migration.

After three, four years of two-day visits,
The message seemed identical with Yeats's wild swans'—
Mortality, mine; that chances were fair
A bird as fragile as a cuckoo clock might
(Despite yearly odysseys through air thick
With threat, toward waters jelled with poison)
Outlast iron me, revisit this pond
In my total absence. Or even the reverse—

Yeats again, *Lapis Lazuli*:
"Over them flies a long-legged bird,
A symbol of longevity."
—Bird's or mine though?

A year ago it seemed suddenly mine.
He arrived late—mid-January—
One day ahead of a hard cold wave
(Clanging air, foot of snow, pond dense as ingots)
And stood on the surface, staring at fish
Safe as houses from what I assumed was
Desperate need. Or took slow
Aimless steps, maladroit as
A nineteenth-century German child's
Toy, all gears and contingency—
First *this*, then *that*. And wouldn't leave—
Waited four, five days as the weather screwed down:
Zero for the first time in my life here.
Mornings I'd come down to see him there,
Condensed a notch farther by night, famine
But hunting still—fish roared in joy,
Their own only enemies. By then his plight
Seemed roughly mine—vital provisions
In clean showcases, permanently sealed—
So I tried to let him at them: coated, booted
Myself and fumbled with a log to stave
A usable hole in the ice. Sealed
Also. All I managed was scaring him
Out of sight (slow agonized ascent,
Unlikely, ludicrous as the doomed Ornithopter).
Two brief consolations—that mere exercise might
Warm him a little; that maybe
He was gone on finally, roused by my impotence
From some odd equinoctial daze—
Fish under glass!—and packed off to Georgia
Or the Everglades.

No. Next morning (sixth day of the freeze)
He was not on view, but when I got home

At five o'clock—light nearly dead—he was
There on thicker ice, stiffer, shrunk,
Bitter as a cast-iron flamingo,
Facing me. Seeing what?
Transmitting what signal? *Hunger to death.*

Plea or command?
Plea I decided and took from my freezer
A twenty-inch trout (gift from a friend's
Weekend in the Smokies), stiff as cordwood,
And thawed it in the oven—instant stench
Which the furniture blotted for slow release.
Then I suited up again and moved down toward him
Gingerly (my normal mode though
I'm awful at it, scare a number of targets—
Was he here to teach that? a hunter's
Tread?). He seemed to watch me head-on
From the center where he stood suspended over
Twelve feet of water; but if he saw,
He'd abandoned fear as a luxury—
Better to risk this absurd approach
Than exert one calorie of life on flight.
I stopped at the edge though the water would have borne
Me as easily as him, stooped and slid
The trout toward him, bowled it perfectly
A foot from his feet, then gingerly left—
Not looking back on my charity, his gratitude
Till indoors again behind my own glass.
He was there, unmoved, facing the trout but
Blind or stupified or too weak
To eat or had to have water
To lubricate a swallow or didn't like trout.
I watched long enough to register nightfall—
I could stand another ten minutes,
Watch him folded in darkness
Or fix my own supper (less desirable than trout)
Or take quilts out to bundle him up,
Force-feed him before his own supper
Froze again.

89

*

I ate, watched the news; and by early
Morning he was still out of sight,
No sign of the trout though—hopeful omen—
Yet after coffee I went down to check.
From my end of the snowy ice to where he'd
Last stood were crowded dog tracks
And, on his site, a small handful
Of lilac-gray feathers. No beak, no bone
Of bird or trout. I'd only succeeded
In luring the neighborhood clutch of hyenas,
Standard lethal suburban equipment.
I knelt for a feather—strong wing
Vane—and thought if that was the meaning,
The message straining through years for delivery,
Then it came as no news, cliché oily
As an oleograph moonrise. Why should nature labor
Through staggering waste to state in mammoth
Semaphore the conclusion any
Baby draws once it's cleared the sphincter
Vaginalis?—*We tear what we touch.*
I dropped the feather and climbed home,
Satisfied.

A normal year passed—normal quota of reminders
That the sentence held (some devious
And eloquent, all wasteful as
The heron episode).

He rises from death. Here anyhow
He stands, eleven months later
In the shallows at my end, facing
Me plainly. What am I meant
To do with my first exposure
To resurrection, at year's dead end,
Before my breakfast? (I manage to recall
That resurrections, like natural births,
Have a habit of dawning in the pre-breakfast

Deserts, roses aghast.) First,
I tell myself it's an accident—
A similar bird on the same flight-path.
That holds me long enough to boil a kettle,
But then I remember a way of establishing
Whether I'm confronted by chance or worse—
By a serious note sounded on air
Clear enough to bear it straight at my eyes,
When I've twiddled these chinking metaphors
(Mortality, Immortality) ten years.
My old heron had something wrong with
His knee (is it called a knee? elbow?
Wrist?)—a knot or tumor
Size of a walnut, stained darker
Than the leg. I decide not to check
Precipitously. In fact, I don't
Look out again. I have my breakfast,
Then carefully search *Britannica*
For firm ground to stand on—
Life span of the great blue heron,
Migration. There's ample word on plumage,
Distribution, abundance ("Herons are the most
Cosmopolitan family"), relations with man
("Members of this order are considered to be
Either beneficial or neutral in respect
To the human economy"), feeding habits,
Vocalization ("Many of the ciconiiforms
Are rather silent," which comes as relief—
The chance mine may speak has seemed
At least even); but no help
At all on maximum age, senility
Or the wintering routes of Atlantic
Seaboard members of the family. What is
Unexpected is the constant reference to
Family—"An outstanding feature
In ciconiiform behaviour is gregariousness.
Even when the mode of obtaining food
Necessitates solitude . . . the tendency is

For reassembly at the end of day"
Though mine, or the long succession of mine,
Stays through nights however arctic:
Loyal, alone, next to me.

Hatted and scarfed, I finally look—
He hasn't moved a visible atom
In forty-five minutes. And doesn't move as
The door slams shut and I start
Toward him. But he's watching me,
Not water or the road—unless he's blind
Or some flawless decoy or angel
Or demon or symptom of lunacy; mine,
At last. I walk to within twenty yards
Of the pond—normal racket of dry leaves,
Sticks. At the noise, I know I'm volunteering,
Offering myself for whatever's next
(Which later will sound like symptom number-two
But then—in bristling winter light
By four still acres of cold
Brown water ringed with chalk-
White bones of sycamores,
Sepulchral cedars—was the rational course).
I walk on. He has the knot on his right
Knee. It's grown—size of an oak
Gall now; is it killing him?
With a speed, calm as perfect, his head
Leaves me, flings out from its coil,
Pierces water silently and rises with
A five-inch brim, lets it quiver
In my sight an instant, eats it.
So I step forward another five yards;
And he bears the nearness for maybe four seconds,
Profile to me. Credible angel—
He gives a first wide fan of wings;
Then rises, trailing legs like crutches.
Till he's half-gone, I hear his oaring
Like lashes—*hrr, hrr*: no pain
Ensues.

*

So left with that—actual phoenix
At the edge of my yard, possessed of new
Grace since his nocturnal skirmish with
The local dingoes; entirely acceptable
Minister of silence—I climb to the otherwise
Empty house and make for myself
An oracle from his mute persistence
Through volumes of air, corrosive years—
Endurance is fed: here, in time.
Therefore endure. Then make another—
You hope in vain. The heart is fed
Only where I go when I leave you here.
Follow me.

REYNOLDS PRICE

Born in Macon, North Carolina in 1933, Reynolds Price attended North Carolina schools and received his Bachelor of Arts degree from Duke University. As a Rhodes Scholar he studied for three years at Merton College, Oxford, receiving the Bachelor of Letters with a thesis on Milton. In 1958 he returned to Duke where he is now James B. Duke Professor of English. His first novel *A Long and Happy Life* appeared in 1962. A volume of stories *The Names and Faces of Heroes* appeared in 1963. In the years since, he has published *A Generous Man* (a novel), *Love and Work* (a novel), *Permanent Errors* (stories), *Things Themselves* (essays and scenes), *The Surface of Earth* (a novel), *Early Dark* (a play), *A Palpable God* (translations from the Bible with an essay on the origins and life of narrative), and *The Source of Light* (a novel). His play for television *Private Contentment* appeared on PBS's "American Playhouse" in 1982. His books have been translated into fourteen languages.